Animals

Copyright © 1988, Raintree Publishers Limited Partnership

Translated by Alison Taurel

**First published as
LES ANIMAUX et leur secrets
by Georgette Barthelemy
Illustrations: J. Reschofsky**

© Editions Fernand Nathan, Paris

Library of Congress Number: 87-28712

3 4 5 6 7 8 9 0   91 90 89

Printed and bound in the United States of America.

Library of Congress Cataloging in Publication Data

Animals.

  (Science and its secrets)
  Includes index.
  Summary: Introduces many kinds of animals, their habits
and behavior, and their relationship with man.
   1. Animals—Juvenile literature. [1. Animals] I. Series.
QL49.A587   1988   591—dc19   87-28712
ISBN 0-8172-3083-1 (lib. bdg.)
ISBN 0-8172-3089-0 (softcover)

PHOTOGRAPHY CREDITS

Cover Photo: Hermines **(Visage-Jacana). Atlas-Photo:** Baron: 30 bottom; Fatras:
58; Frederik: 48; Lauros: 22; Nuridsany: 30 top; Schultz: 50 right. **Holmes-Lebel:**
27 bottom, 60; Meyers: 14 Schumacher: 19. **Jacana:** Dupont: 27 top; Frederik: 8
bottom; Lanceau: 25, 38 top; Nikon: 21; Tercafs: 20, 44; Visage: 13. **Pitch:** Bernard:
16 top right; Binois: 34 top; Bourret: 40 bottom left; Chantelat: 47, 52; Chapelain:
59; Montoya: 10, 11, 29 bottom, 36 bottom, 40 top, 45, 49, 50 left; Patel: 37 top, 37
bottom right; Peuriot: 46; Prissette: 33 top; Rainon: 28; Schrempp: 7, 9 bottom, 26
top, 35, 37 bottom; Vienne-Bel: 16 top left, 16 bottom, 23 top, 24 top, 24 bottom,
43 top, 51 center, 51 bottom, 53, 57 top. **Rapho:** Spiegel: 43 bottom; Starosta: 8
top, 9 top, 12, 17, 26 bottom, 29 top and center; 31 top and bottom, 32, 36 top, 38
bottom, 41, 42, 56, 61.

ANIMALS

Raintree Publishers — Milwaukee

Contents

THE ANIMAL WORLD

Alpine marmots.

What is meant by an animal species?

Two related species—a donkey and a horse.

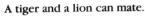

A tiger and a lion can mate.

Animals (and plants) are grouped into categories known as kingdoms, phyla, classes, orders, families, genera, and species. *Species* is a basic unit of scientific classification.

When a cow and a horse are observed, it is not too difficult to see that they are two very different animals. But when observing a German shepherd and a Pekingese, it may be hard to tell that they belong to the same species.

A *species* is a group of living beings with one *lineage* among them. Members of a species breed with one another. Under natural circumstances, one species usually does not breed with another.

There exists a natural barrier between the species which prevents them from crossing.

In each cell of all beings there is a sort of program of makeup. This program varies from one individual to another. But in the same species, the variations are not sufficiently important to prevent the union of two beings. The result is the formation of a new being.

Young roosters and hens are the offspring of roosters and hens. They will become adult roosters and hens and have their own chicks. Ducks and chickens cannot have eggs together. The difference in their programs is too big. They cannot cross the barrier.

However, as with all rules, there are exceptions. The horse and the donkey may be crossed, and their offspring is the mule. The lion and the tiger can have tigrons.

Why are there more land animals than marine animals?

Every living being has its environmental preference. The carp loves calm waters, and the trout loves rough waters. The poplar grows in humid soil, while some pine trees prefer sandy, dry soil. The chestnut cannot grow in soil with limestone, while other trees prefer it. The antelope lives in the warm African savanna, while the polar bear prefers a cold climate.

There is an infinite variety of living conditions on land and in warm waters as evidenced by the many different elevations and soils.

Despite the greatness of the oceans, the variety of conditions is much smaller than on land. The winds, the rains, and the dryness do not exist for marine animals. Salt content may vary depending on the particular ocean. On land, however, the composition of soils may change several times over a small area. Although life first appeared in the oceans, it is on land and in the skies that it shows the greatest variety.

The Alpine ibex loves scaling mountains and heights.

How do new species appear?

Changes in heredity and natural selection contribute to the appearance of new animal and vegetable species. Climatic changes explain the appearance and disappearance of animals and plants.

On the long road of drought, the herd stretches out, fatigued.

More than five million years ago, an immense cone rose out of the Pacific Ocean. It was the first of the islands in the Hawaiian Islands. It was visited by tiny fruit flies (drosophila), carried more by the wind than by their wings.

Naturalists who studied the first of these flies in Hawaii had quite a surprise. Isolated from other lands, the small flies became enormous flies showing very different characteristics than their very, very ancient ancestors. Evidently, they are incapable of crossing with any other species of drosophiles.

The story of the Hawaiian fruit flies shows us how new animal or vegetable species are formed. The isolation of a small group of living beings in a habitat that is well defined by its climate, its relief, and other organisms which occupy it, slowly modifies their hereditary program. This very slow modification is due to a natural choice of the individuals best adapted to the conditions. New characteristics appear, while old traits disappear. In time, a new species is created, isolated from the first by a different program.

Following a terrible drought, a horde of herbivorous animals flees the region it had inhabited up until then. During the voyage, numerous animals die of hunger and thirst. The most resistant reach a less desolate land. Other grass-eaters have preceded them. The fight for food is bitter. One of the animals from the herd has a young one which has a big advantage over the others. Its neck, longer than normal, makes it possible for it to get leaves inaccessible to its companions. Why was it born with a longer neck? It was most certainly an accident in the development of its hereditary program and this accident was, in turn, transmitted to some of its offspring. Those which had longer necks lived longer than the others. They then had many descendants. Bit by bit, the shorter necked animals disappeared and among the "long necks," the longest of them had the best chance of living. At the same time, these herbivores developed a greater and greater resistance to drought. There came a time when the length of the neck stabilized because necks that were too long were as useless as necks that were too short.

That is the story of giraffes, animals with long necks that can go without drinking for a week or more. But how much time passed between the thirsty animal at the beginning and the giraffe such as we know it today? Regarding changes in the species, the unit of time most often used is in millions of years!

A reticulated giraffe from the north of Somalia in Africa.

A small giraffe will become big. Like its mother, it will reach the highest branches. Long necks allow giraffes to exist in a semi-desert climate, reaching the branches that are inaccessible to other animals.

11

How are animals named?

Several years ago a team of scientists paid a visit to some tribes of New Guinea who had never before had contact with our civilization. They lived with them for several weeks.

The natives were very knowledgeable about the plants and animals which surrounded them, which was not surprising. What was a surprise was that of the two hundred species of birds, the natives knew the difference between some very similar species and had actually given each species two names, just like the zoologists! Obviously, they were not Latin names, but there were two.

In order to name animals, zoologists have the custom of using two names of Latin or Greek origin. Latin and Greek words are used in scientific classification because early scholars were masters of these languages.

The first name always begins with a capital letter. That is the *genus*—a group of animals having common characteristics. Genus consists of similar groups, but members of the groups do not breed with each other. The genus *Canis* includes the coyote and the timber wolf. Coyotes and timber wolves, however, ordinarily do not breed with each other.

The second name is written entirely in small letters, and it is the name of the species. Members of a species have several common characteristics, but they differ in one or more ways. Members of a species can breed with each other. No two species in a genus have the same scientific name. Canis latrans is the coyote. Canis lupus is the timber wolf.

The lion's scientific name is Panthera leo. The tiger, its cousin, is the Panthera tigris.

The lion and tiger are of the same genus but of different species.

Sometimes, a third name is added, particularly in the case of insects which are so numerous and so delicate to classify.

Why do scientists use Latin or Greek names?

Latin and old Greek were languages commonly used in the sciences. Moreover, the use of Latin and Greek allowed scientists to understand each other, whether they were French, German, or Russian.

How are the names chosen?

Often, they are the translations of the common name—*leo* means lion in Latin. They may also reflect a particular aspect of the animal. Pteroceros are species of marine snails that have shells that flare out into a wing decorated with horns (*pteron:* wing, *ceros:* horn). Sometimes, a species will be named after a scientist.

A name for a new species is always chosen carefully because the proposed name must be known all over the world.

Pterocere rugueux. The girth of certain specimens may be more than 7 inches (20 cm).

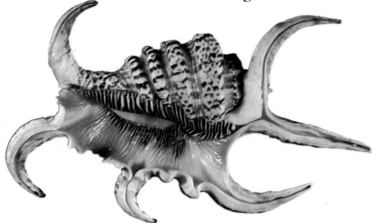

ANIMAL CURIOSITIES

At autumn's onset, ermines change their brownish fur to white.

What is the largest of all the animals on the planet?

The largest animal of all is the blue whale. It is the largest animal that has ever existed on the earth. It can reach 100 feet (30 meters) long and weigh over 100 short tons (91 metric tons).

How did the whale manage to become so huge?

This enormous mammal lives in the sea, and the sea nourishes it. With a lot of food and the support of the water, it could not help but become enormous. The heaviest of all land animals today is the African elephant, whose four powerful feet support up to eight tons. It is exceeded in weight by some fish like the shark-whale, which can weigh as much as twelve tons.

Land animals cannot develop too large or else they will die from their own weight. A beached whale dies crushed by the weight of its own skin. The huge brontosaurus lived most of the time in swamps where it could find the necessary support for its massive weight.

A beautiful baby!

The largest of all animals, the blue whale, also has the biggest babies weighing from two to three tons at birth. At birth, babies are about 23 feet (7 meters) long and grow by about 220 pounds (100 kilograms) a day. A newborn human infant gains about an ounce (30 grams) a day.

A brontosaurus grazing.

What are the smallest animals? The fastest?

The smallest of all animals were also the first living beings. They are found at the base of the animal scale. Just as the life of a person begins with a tiny, unique cell, the animal kingdom began to be distinguished by unicellular beings called *protozoa*.

There were numerous quarrels among botanists and zoologists on the subject of certain protozoa. Certain species actually show characteristics of both kingdoms as if there had been, right at the start of the split between living things, a hesitation between animal or vegetable life.

The fastest animals

Birds are the fastest animals. The duck hawk is the very fastest, reaching 180 miles (290 km) per hour. The golden eagle travels at 120 miles (193 km) per hour.

ANIMAL	SPEED	
Cheetah	70 mph	(110 kph)
Hummingbird	60 mph	(97 kph)
Gazelle	50 mph	(80 kph)
House cat	30 mph	(48 kph)
Barracuda	30 mph	(48 kph)
Sailfish	30 mph	(48 kph)
Dolphin	25 mph	(40 kph)
People (running)	20 mph	(32 kph)
Housefly	5 mph	(8 kph)
People (swimming)	5 mph	(8 kph)
Goldfish	4 mph	(6 kph)
Turtle	1/10 mph	(.16 kph)

A colony of paramecia.

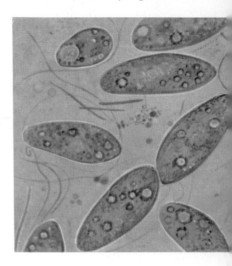

A pecking ostrich.

An albatross about to take off.

Which is the biggest bird?

An Andean condor.

The largest and heaviest of the birds is obviously the ostrich with its height of 8 feet (2.5 m) and its 330 pounds (150 kg). But it is a bird that does not fly. In contrast, it runs very quickly and can easily attain speeds of 37 miles (60 km) per hour. Its wings are ridiculously small, and they barely serve to help balance the ostrich when it runs.

Among birds that fly, two species vie for the biggest—the albatross and the Andean condor.

The albatross is a magnificent bird of the high seas. An incomparable glider, it only touches ground to lay eggs and raise its young. It sleeps while gliding in air currents and feeds on marine animals. Its body is white and about 47 inches (120 centimeters) long from the tip of its beak to the end of its tail. Its tapered wings have black tips. Its wingspan is 13 feet (4 m)!

The Andean condor is a scavenger of the vulture family. It is also an excellent glider but with very wide wings. It mostly lives on decaying flesh. Its head and throat are without feathers. Vultures are very useful animals, as are all scavengers. Its slow, circling flight is incredible to see.

What is the largest insect?

The largest of all insects is the Goliath. It is an animal in the same group as maybugs and ladybugs. As with all insects, it has a hard shell on the head and thorax. The fine, membranous wings fold under thick shields, which make protective cases when the Goliath is at rest.

The Goliath can weigh 3.5 ounces (100 grams). It measures 4 inches (10 cm) in length and 8 inches (20 cm) in width when it spreads its wings.

These creatures have a very different breathing and circulation system than humans. Holes pierced in their shells communicate with small canals which branch out to the muscles and circulate oxygen. The areas of the muscles that are near to the respiratory canals are well oxygenated. The areas farther away receive less oxygen.

All the organs are situated in the blood which nourishes them. A little oxygen passes through the walls of the respiratory canals in the blood, but it can only hold a small amount. This distribution of air is sufficient for a small organism, but it would be defective in a larger animal.

A long time ago, before people appeared on earth, there was a kind of ladybug which had a wingspan of about 27 inches (70 cm). Although it was larger than the Goliath, it had a much slimmer body.

The Goliath gathers nectar from flowers that are found at the tops of large trees in central Africa. It makes a lot of noise when it flies. Its larva is a fat, white worm with six feet like the maybug.

A giant beetle: the Goliath.

When the Goliath gathers nectar, it acts like a helicopter that buzzes around the flowers!

What is the "strangest" of the mammals?

Endowed with a shell that makes it resemble a tortoise, the armadillo is an extraordinary animal. Nevertheless, in spite of its double armor of horny, bony scales which provide it with a veritable external skeleton, it is a mammal.

Armadillos are burrowing animals, and they live under the ground. They hunt at night. They behave similarly to the hedgehog. Both the hedgehog and the armadillo possess the ability to roll themselves into a ball when faced with danger. The bony armor can protect the vulnerable underparts.

With its strange appearance, the armadillo seems to have come down through the ages to us. It is a descendant of a common ancestor of the enormous *glyptodon,* whose shells were used as dwellings for the first inhabitants of South America. It has primitive characteristics which place it in a strange family, that of the *Edentata.*

A "toothy" edentate

Edentate animals are toothless. This family is a sort of hold-all in which zoologists, who classify mammals according to the shape and distribution of their teeth, put all those creatures that do not correspond to the established norms. For an animal that is classified as an edentate, the armadillo is quite lucky. It has from twenty-eight to one hundred small teeth.

The armadillo has survived because it has great ease of adaptation. Having discovered garbage dumps (which are rich in food waste) several years ago, it has spread considerably over the United States, even reaching the Canadian border. This "prehistoric creature" has found a way to flourish in modern times.

> The armadillo has no border to its hunting grounds. It roams at night in search of insects and waste. Its burrow is several feet deep. That is where it rests during the day.

An armadillo in search of its burrow.

ANIMAL LIFE

A happy pack of bathing raccoons.

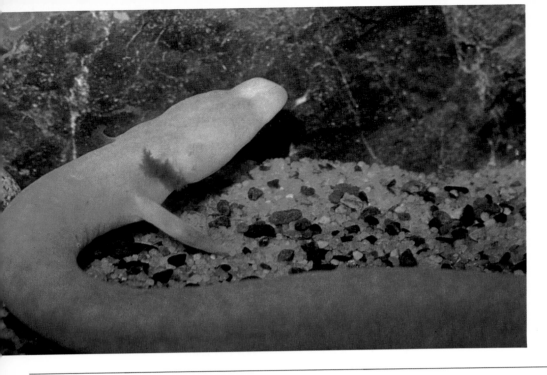

This amphibian larva is blind and lives in a cave.

Can animals live without light?

Yes, animals can live without light. In great watery depths where the sun's rays cannot penetrate, there are small, strangely-shaped fish. But they make their own light by secreting phosphorescent mucus. In addition, their eyes are very developed to seize even the slightest signs of light announcing the presence of a fellow creature.

In caverns, the darkness is total. The majority of animals that live in caves are only temporary guests. Bats, of which there may be thousands living in one cave, go out at night to hunt insects. Small rodents gladly take refuge under ground, only coming out to eat at night.

But there are insects, some crustaceans, worms, spiders, fish, and batrachians (vertebrate amphibians) who live perpetually in the dark. They are all blind and lack pigmentation. Almost transparent, they live by devouring each other.

As far as batrachians are concerned, the transformation from larva into adult can only take place if the thyroid gland receives some vibrations of light.

Without light, life is possible. But it presents a limited range of forms that vary little and are often incomplete and underdeveloped.

Strictly *cavernal* animals have been, at some point in their history, beings that lived in the sunlight. But since being enclosed in caverns with no way of getting out, they have adapted themselves to this life without light. They acquired senses that make it possible for them to move about and hunt without seeing, and they have lost their useless vision. Their cells have stopped fabricating pigments since the protection which they give against rays of light is pointless.

How do dolphins and whales sleep?

We are quite certain that whales must sleep as do all mammals, birds, and reptiles, but no one has seen a whale sleep. It is very difficult to study the behavior of such large animals. However, dolphins, which are part of the same family, have been observed in captivity.

Apparently, these animals follow the same pattern as most people. They sleep at night and are active in the daytime, with, sometimes, small naps in between.

In calm water, a sleeping dolphin floats, relaxed in its liquid environment. It goes down about a foot (30 cm) below the surface, and every half-minute a gentle movement of the tail brings it back to the surface. The nostril on top of its head opens, and it breathes in air. This up-and-down movement is made unconsciously, without waking the animal. It has been noticed that there is a slight movement of the eyelids which part slightly with each rise to the surface. When the water is rough, the rhythms of surfacing become more rapid, and the swishes of the tail are more vigorous.

This dolphin floats on the surface in the warmth of the sun.

Why do some animals sleep all winter?

A hibernating bat is startled by the photographer's flash.

In caves in winter, bats by the hundreds hang upside down with their wings folded.

In a nest in the hollow of a thicket, the American ground squirrel is curled up in a ball under the snow.

The marmot is immobile for six months of the year in its burrow under the cold rocks.

As soon as the cold arrives, the brown bear buries itself in the ferns and leaves it has accumulated. All these animals seem to sleep, numbed by the cold.

Are they really sleeping?

Yes, they are in a state of hibernation or inactivity.

When people sleep, breathing is a little slower, and internal body temperature lowers a small amount. No matter how deep people are in sleep, it normally lasts no longer than ten to twelve hours. Hunger awakens people.

Bats and ground squirrels have a much different sleep than people. The rhythm of their heartbeats is very slowed down. Hunger does not awaken them because they are living at a slower pace. There is a very great reduction of the vital functions. Fat accumulated during summertime is used by the marmot to maintain a reasonable temperature. The animal loses a quarter of its weight during its long sleep.

"True" hibernation happens only to warm-blooded animals. In true hibernation, the animal's body temperature falls close to the temperature of the surrounding air. Another type of hibernation happens to cold-blooded animals. Butterflies and moths hibernate by changing from a caterpillar into a pupa (cocoon). Frogs, lizards, snakes, toads, and turtles "cool down" as winter approaches. During the very cold season, their body processes almost stop.

Bears do not hibernate in the true sense. They sleep through the winter, but their body temperatures do not drop much below normal.

Some bats hibernate every day and become active again every night. Certain hummingbirds hibernate each night. Some animals slow their body processes down in summer when water is scarce.

Does the cold bring about this sleepiness?

Yes, the cold is a major cause. As soon as the weather warms, the animals wake up. Hibernation is a way for animals to defend themselves against conditions that are too harsh. During hibernation, the animals' vital forces are economized as much as possible.

Can all mammals enter this lethargic state?

Only certain families of mammals have this ability. Zoologists have classified mammals according to their need to maintain a constant internal temperature. There are those for whom this need is imperative—if their body temperatures lower, they die. This is the case with people and dogs. There are animals that can easily support a lower temperature, but they will not accept it unless forced to, as is the case with rats and mice.

This brown bear was awakened before the end of the winter. He will not be able to go back to sleep again.

The Alpine marmot, waking from his lethargic rest, comes out of his burrow.

23

A red stag and family.

The young, downy antlers of a roe deer.

Do female deer have antlers?

Antlers are limited to the male among most species of deer. Only female reindeer and caribou have these magnificent horns called antlers. The antlers do not stay all year through, however.

Every year, at the end of winter, deer lose their antlers. They do not grow back again until summer at the time of reproduction.

Antlers grow from permanent knobby bones on the deer's head. When the antlers reappear, they are covered with a very soft, velvety skin that has fine blood vessels running through it. This skin then dries out and the animal scratches itself against tree trunks to scrape off these shreds.

Deer use their antlers mainly to fight for water or for leadership of the herd.

The musk deer of Asia and the Chinese water deer do not have antlers.

Is it possible to tell the age of a deer by looking at the antlers?

The age and health of a deer can be determined through the antlers. The first set grows when the deer is one or two years old.

A young, year-old deer has only one branch of antlers. Each year he will gain one more point or antler, until his antlers attain their fully developed state. Depending on the species, there are six to ten antlers.

What is inside the camel's hump?

A camel or a dromedary can go for eight days without drinking if it is neither overloaded nor made to take long trips. Obviously, after such treatment, it must "renew" its hump and fill up with water. The camel has two humps, and the dromedary has one.

The "ships of the desert" as these animals are sometimes called are animals that are perfectly adapted to life in desert regions. Humid countries are unhealthy for them.

Moving on sand most of the time, they have no hooves but rather claws under which there are fat cushions. Their toes can thus spread out like paddles to facilitate their walking on loose soil.

And finally, everything in the camel's body has evolved to make it possible for it to resist drought.

In deserts, the air may contain a large amount of water vapor (water transformed into gas). The desert atmosphere literally "pumps" all the water it can find, whether from soil or from living beings, and transforms it into vapor. This drying air does not affect camels and dromedaries. They do not perspire and a particularly thick, woolly fleece on their backs protects them from drying out. If they need water, they find it in their own bodies.

Pockets of water

The camel's stomach is made up of several parts. One of them contains "pockets of water" closed by muscles that can open when the need arises. People in caravans have quenched their thirst by killing their camel to drink the water from its stomach!

The humps are actually large masses of fat. Practically all the fat that may accumulate in the animal is found in these humps. These fatty masses have a double advantage. They are used for both nourishment and water reserve. Thanks to special enzymes, the fat may be partially transformed into water when the stomach's reservoirs are empty.

A dromedary renews his hump.

How do polecats and skunks defend themselves?

When an animal is small and seemingly defenseless or hungry and food is hard to find, there is an excellent way to deal with the situation—scare the other animals away. That is what polecats and skunks do by releasing a horrible odor.

As soon as one of these small carnivores is frightened or angry, it turns its back, lifts up its tail, and squirts a nauseating and irritating liquid. If this liquid comes into contact with the eyes of an animal, the animal becomes temporarily blinded.

Many skunks live in underground dens lined with leaves. The spotted skunk is able to climb and, therefore, can live in hollow trees. Skunks sleep during the day and search for food at night. They sleep for weeks at a time during winter. Skunks don't have many enemies, but great horned owls and bobcats will attack them regardless of the terrible odor.

Like skunks, polecats live in the ground or in trees. The polecat hunts at night and stores extra food.

A surprised polecat emits an awful smell.

This African zoril with black stripes resembles its cousin, the American skunk.

Does an eagle really have extraordinary eyesight?

An "eagle eye" is what a person with particularly good eyesight is called. However, no matter how good a human's eyesight is, it can never compare to that of this bird of prey.

All birds are blessed with great visual capacity. They are the animals which depend the most on sight. They live in the air and have to locate their nourishment, their territory, and their enemies as quickly as possible. Compared to their overall size, their eyes are very large. Birds' eyes are very different from people's eyes. People only see well when objects are almost directly in line with their pupils. Birds have a much broader field of vision.

In the case of birds of prey like the eagle, the eye is very deep, almost tubular. Because of this, the image on the retina is much larger. That enables the animal to distinguish details more accurately.

Their color vision is very well developed and assists their keen perception of detail even more.

At an altitude of 330 feet (100 m), an eagle is capable of distinguishing two points separated by less than half an inch (1 cm).

In birds, each eye has distinct vision. The vision of the two eyes is never combined, as with people, into a single image. Bearing this in mind, they should, in fact, have poor judgement of distances. As this is not the case, it must be because they have other ways of seeing. No doubt their tremendous eyesight is assisted by the comb-shaped crest which juts out above the retina and which is particularly developed in the bird of prey's eye.

The piercing look of the eagle and its majestic flight.

Are hummingbirds really the size of houseflies?

Compare the size of the flower to that of the bird.

Hummingbirds live only in the Western Hemisphere. More than four hundred kinds are known, but the bee hummingbird (which is found in Cuba) is the smallest bird in the world. It is about 2 inches (5 cm) long, including the beak and tail. It weighs .07 ounces (2 grams). No fly gets up to this size, but butterflies do. There are many insects that are larger than hummingbirds, too.

Extraordinary flight!

Its flight justifies the hummingbird's name. Seventy beats of its wings per second make it hum like a fly. Capable of hovering like a helicopter, it can also fly backward as well as forward, a unique feat in the bird world.

This tiny animal is warm-blooded as are all birds. Whatever the outside temperature, the internal temperature of the hummingbird does not vary and remains in the area of 107.6°F (42°C).

In order to compensate for the cold, the hummingbird must constantly remain in motion. Since it needs to provide food for its muscles to create so much movement, it must eat almost constantly. The hummingbird, size notwithstanding, is a big eater. It hunts insects, but its main meal is nectar from flowers. According to scientists, the size of this bird is the very smallest a warm-blooded creature can be.

The largest hummingbird is the giant hummer found in the Andes Mountains of South America. It grows to a length of 9 inches (23 cm).

Nineteen types of hummingbirds make their homes in the United States. Most are found in the western and southwestern states.

Why do lizards lose their tails?

A lizard is lying on a rock. It is taking advantage of the sun's warmth. The skin on its neck beats gently to the rhythm of its breathing. It is warm and happy.

At the slightest noise, it slides at full speed to hide under stones. An attacker might be quicker, but if a lizard is caught by the tail, the tail will detach.

This is painful to the lizard, but it would rather lose its tail than lose its life. In the middle of its tail is a coil-shaped muscle which is strong enough to break the vertebrae by contracting. The traction used by the attacker is enough to finish off the amputation. This tail will grow anew at least one time.

The twitching of the end of the detached tail can distract the attention of the enemy. In fact, the tail continues to move for several moments after it is detached.

A sleeping gecko, with its tail.

A gecko awake, without its tail!

A richly-colored male agama. They can be found in tropical Africa.

How do insects get through the winter?

A nest of wasps. Notice the eggs inside the cells.

In the winter, when it is cold, flies and mosquitoes disappear. Butterflies have long fled the flowerless gardens. Forget about seeing an aphid, a grasshopper, or a bee. Where have they gone?

Fleeing the cold, great swarms of insects fly toward the warmer spots on the globe. Flies, ladybugs, and butterflies travel together. Helped along by the winds, they pass over mountains and seas. Many die on the way. The strongest make it to their wintering spot, where it is warm and food is abundant. In spring, they will return to their summer environment.

Not all insects migrate. Some bury themselves deep in the ground where they are sheltered from the frost. They hibernate there just like bears and marmots. Hibernation is a very practical way of passing the cold weather season for some animals. As soon as the animal feels the cold, it starts to live at a slower pace. Its vital needs are reduced to a strict minimum. It doesn't feed or excrete

any longer and seems to fall into a deep sleep. With insects, this numbness that takes place when all vital functions are suspended is called diapause. Certain butterflies pass the winter hidden this way in bushes, hollow trees, or old walls. It's not unusual to find hibernating ladybugs hidden in the folds of curtains in houses in the country. Ants in anthills and bees in beehives go into diapause at the first sign of cold weather.

Many insects die before the end of summer. Most of them have only a brief adult life. The adult stage in insects is that of reproduction. When the eggs have been laid, the insect disappears. Eggs can exist through winter and hatch in spring, or the hatching may take place before winter. The adult maybug has a brief life of about three weeks. In autumn, the larvae which come out of the eggs laid in the soil travel almost 2 feet (60 cm) into the ground. In the spring, the larvae come out of their numbness and climb close to the surface where they find edible roots. Larvae will pass two years like this. At the beginning of the third year when shedding has taken place, the insects have become maybugs and go to live their short aerial lives. As soon as the weather starts to cool, aphids start laying eggs with stronger shells, different from those in summer and which hatch very quickly. Aphids die in the first frosts, but their eggs will hatch in spring.

Certain solitary bees hollow out a small tunnel in the earth and enclose their eggs there, along with a layer of pollen and honey which the larvae will eat upon hatching.

Wild bees in full activity on their honeycomb.

Do insects feel pain the way people do?

Insects' nervous systems are very different from those of human beings. People have a brain and a spinal cord from which the nerves go forth. Insects have a nervous system which consists of a brain and two nerve cords. These nerve cords run the length of an insect's body. The brain receives information from the eyes and antennae. It also controls the insect's body as a whole. But the brain is not the only command post of the insect's movements. It is also not the only outcome of the messages of the organs and senses. Instead, certain activities are read and controlled at points along the nerve cords. At these points, each of the two cords contains a cluster of nerve cells. These nerve centers are called ganglions. One ganglion, found in the head, is organized in a circle around the mouth parts. But ganglions also occur in each segment of the thorax and abdomen— one on each cord. The two ganglions in each section are fused together. They form a sort of small brain that controls its own segment. They can, in fact, work without the central brain if necessary. For example, in battle, an ant sometimes has its head cut off. The ant continues to walk for a short time. Some such insects have even been known to mate and lay eggs. Both examples are a result of control from ganglions. In most insects, however, the central brain is still the control center.

The sensitive nerves of insects go from their skin to their ganglions. There is no deep sensation. They

A bumblebee searching for nectar.

would not feel pain in their muscles if the muscles were cut off. But their exterior sensitivity is very well developed. The hairs which cover their hard, horny shells are in the nervous system with the ganglions. These hairs are made by skin cells which are found under the protective layer of shell. The hairs pass across the points where the shell is the thinnest. They make it possible for the insect to feel, touch, taste, and hear.

When an insect's feet are injured, it probably does not feel any deep pain. Still, it does feel the hairs that cover its feet being crumpled. This sensation might be compared to what you feel when someone scrapes their fingers across a blackboard. Although the insect may not be in terrible pain, it certainly feels an injury.

People should be careful not to cause an animal undue suffering, no matter what the animal is.

The beautiful, feathery antennae of a moth.

How can a little ant carry an object heavier than it is?

When looking at the soil in summer it is not rare to see one or several ants carrying seeds or pieces of food toward an anthill. Often, the food is very large in comparison to the animal.

The ant could push the seed and make it roll, but it lifts it by using very strong pincers which fold up under its mouth.

The ants who bring in food generally have large heads with powerful mandibles (jaws). The mandibles maintain their grip as solidly as a pair of powerful, grooved tongs.

The animal could be unbalanced by a load that it is carrying, but its three pairs of feet (which end in claws) ensure it an efficient anchoring on the ground. It balances the weight between its head and abdomen.

The ant benefits from a totally different musculature than that of a mammal. The muscles are made of elastic fibers which can, under the command of the nervous system, contract and release. In insects, the contraction is more rapid, more intense. Just think, the wing beats of a fly can attain a rhythm of 200 to 250 beats per second! Insects have no lungs. Air enters their bodies directly by small areas called stigmatas, and their skin bathes in a nutritious liquid. In this manner, muscular fibers are quickly fed with energizing substances.

Fatigue exists among ants as it does with humans. So sometimes ants must let their cargo drop. It is up to other members of the anthill to finish the project.

A major grain-eating worker ant at full steam.

Do some animals escape their enemies with trickery?

Certain animals are not well equipped with means of defense. They have no claws, no teeth, no stings, and no shell. Therefore, these animals have developed other defenses. Mimicry consists of miming or resembling another animal, a plant, or a stone. Common mimics include butterflies, hover flies, beetles, and flies that look like bees. When an insect mimics another, as in the last example, the model insect often has protective devices. These devices may include stings, pinches, or foul odors. Such is the case of the viceroy butterfly. This butterfly closely resembles the monarch butterfly. Both have bright wing patterns. But the monarch has a very unpleasant taste. Any bird that has ever tried eating one will not attack another. This protects the viceroy, which does not have an unpleasant taste. Because the viceroy looks like the monarch, birds and other predators will leave it alone.

Of course, one insect does not set out to imitate the other. The viceroy does not choose to look like the monarch. Rather, this change takes place over time.

Above: A good example of mimicry—this butterfly looks like a dead leaf.

Right: A swallowtail.

Below: A walking stick.

Stick-like animals

Walking sticks are insects that have developed a great resemblance to the world of vegetation which surrounds them. Certain species are very similar to twigs, others to leaves. But among those which mimic sticks, some are capable of stiffening themselves and staying immobile like the branch they are imitating. At the slightest suspicious movement, the animal becomes rigid like a true stick.

A colony of waterfowl stops at the edge of a pond.

How are swamps useful to animals?

A group of tadpoles.

Swamps are areas of wet, muddy, often low land covered by trees and shrubs. They are found throughout the world in areas along coasts, near slow-flowing rivers, etc. If you have ever passed near a swamp in warm weather, you know swamps often have unpleasant odors. Despite this, swamps are very important to the balance of nature. It is important that these areas be maintained.

For one thing, the stagnant water found in swamps is rich in microscopic organisms. These organisms are a choice food for fish or the creatures on which they feed. By eliminating these areas, the natural equilibrium of nature would be disturbed.

In their soils, swamps shelter a large number of animals. Some of them pass their larval stage there. Frogs and toads, which are great consumers of harmful insects, lay their eggs in swamps. The tadpoles which hatch from these eggs swim in the ponds until their metamorphosis.

These dormant waters also serve sometimes as resting areas for aquatic and migratory birds.

They are refuge stations for numerous species.

Worms, crustaceans, fish, batrachians, reptiles, birds, and quite a few mammals live in the swamps. Others survive because of the swamps.

Swamps are the source of biological riches. They must be protected.

ANIMALS' FOOD

A carnivorous marsupial, the opossum.

Which are the hunters, and which are the hunted?

Processionary pine tree caterpillars . . . in a procession!

The natural balance of animal life in a region depends on many things. One of them is the number of predators as compared to the number of prey. Predators are animals that hunt and kill other animals for food. The animals that are hunted are the prey. The shark which eats small fish is a predator of those fish. The small fish are its prey. But those same small fish may eat plankton. The fish are then predators of those organisms.

Predators can feed on many living things. The bear eats berries, honey, small mammals, and fish. By contrast, the ladybug only eats insects which it catches in flight.

The role of predators is very important. It limits overpopulation. The following example is well known to ecologists.

In a particular part of the ocean, sharks and other small fish live. The sharks eat the small fish. When fish are plentiful, there is food for many sharks and their number increases. When the sharks are too numerous, the fish diminish in number. Having no more to eat, the sharks die or leave. The fish can then start to increase again.

Certain birds of prey like to eat snakes. That is the case with the secretary bird of South Africa. It has always been protected because its presence is beneficial to the limitation of a number of reptiles. It has an excellent appetite—four to five large snakes generally make up its dinner.

If a species multiplies too greatly, it is because something has kept down the numbers of its natural enemies or that too much food has kept down the competition.

At one time, hawks were considered pests. Hunters and farmers had killed so many hawks that none remained. Soon the farmers' fields were overrun by rodents, which are the hawk's common prey. After trying to control the rodents themselves, the farmers brought a pair of hawks into the area. Before long, the rodent population decreased.

A very useful bird of prey—the secretary bird of South Africa.

The Canadian otter, ready to dive.

Are some animals cruel on purpose?

The ferret, the stone marten, the weasel, and the polecat have bad reputations. They sometimes attack chicken coops. But that is nothing compared to the wonderful service they provide by eating rats, mice, and even snakes. They also limit the number of rabbits. Losing some eggs and chickens is a fair price to pay to be rid of unwanted rats, mice, and snakes.

Birds of prey also had bad reputations for a long time—"poachers of the sky," the hunters said. But in actuality, the prey they hunted was often ill or wounded. Their principal nourishment is made up of unwanted rodents and snakes.

The otter is another example. Otters eat a lot of fish. In some cases, otters can cut a river's fish population to almost nothing. When this happens, many people want the otters to be destroyed. That was actually done once. In the end, the otter was not the problem. In fact, otters are beneficial to fish populations. Consider the fish it eats. An otter swims very well, but not as well as a healthy fish. The fish it does catch and eat are often weak or ill. So when the otters were eliminated, it slowed the process of natural selection. As you may remember, natural selection allows the animals best-suited to an environment to thrive. But for this process to work, the balance of nature must be maintained. When the otters were destroyed, the balance was destroyed. This allowed the diseased fish to survive. In the end, the entire fish population suffered. Today, however, otters are protected. Having otters present will keep the fish population strong.

The stone marten and his pointed muzzle.

37

How do goats make deserts?

These goats don't hesitate to climb a tree to graze on the tender leaves.

In arid and in fertile regions, the goat is very much appreciated by the residents. Not hard to please where the quality of food is concerned, the goat provides milk and one or two young a year for its owner. In areas where the goat does not find anything to graze on, this resourceful creature manages to eat. A meal might consist of leaves, buds that are still hard, tree bark, branches, and paper.

Goats can cause damage with their endless appetites. By clipping everything in their paths, goats destroy the vegetation. Greedy and agile on their small horned feet, they climb in trees to eat the tender shoots. The presence of goats transforms the terrain bit by bit into desert.

In one case, the hungry goats nearly brought destruction to a small village in southern Italy. The goats had destroyed all plant life in the area. The land was useless, and the people were starving. At one point, someone suggested destroying the goats. The poor village people protested. They were poor enough without having their only wealth taken away. But some people knew that the village would be poor as long as the goats thrived. It would only grow more desert-like each day. Finally, the goats were destroyed. With work, the land was irrigated. New trees were planted. Prosperity returned to the village.

What do ladybugs eat?

Ladybug larva eating.

The charming little ladybug is a carnivorous predator. It devours aphids that fall into its path.

In the larval stage as in the adult stage, a ladybug's diet is the same. Moreover, the forward-thinking ladybug lays her eggs on stalks frequented by aphids. Therefore, after hatching, her offspring will begin their feast and will not be menaced by hunger. Aphids have an incredible faculty for reproduction. It has been calculated that if the descendants of just one female aphid all lived through the season, in autumn there would be two hundred tons of aphids!

Fortunately, ladybugs save us from being overpopulated with aphids.

Aphids have needle-shaped oral parts which make it possible for them to pierce stalks down to the vessels where sap circulates. They then inhale the sap. A dozen aphids sucking on a plant in this manner is not serious. But when there are thousands of them, the plant is used up and withers away.

When insecticides are used to kill aphids, the predators (ladybugs) are also in danger of being exterminated at the same time. Unfortunately, aphids get used to poison more quickly than ladybugs do.

Perhaps one day gardeners will buy, not a can of insecticide, but a dozen ladybugs. That would be much more efficient in the long run.

Can an eagle carry off a sheep?

There is nothing sadder than seeing an eagle in a cage. Its powerful talons sink into a ridiculous piece of wood which serves as its perch. Immobile, this magnificent bird, which is used to gliding around the vast sky, looks at visitors with a serious eye.

Some eagles, such as the golden eagle, are fierce predators. Golden eagles prey on rabbits, squirrels, and even young deer and lambs. They can carry prey weighing as much as they do. But other eagles, such as the bald eagle, are not as fierce. The bald eagle eats a lot of fish which it snatches from the water. On occasion, it will even plunge into the water for an instant. Bald eagles also eat many kinds of dead animals. Eagles are also known to eat snakes and lizards. An eagle's diet depends on where it lives.

But because it is a bird of prey, the eagle has a bad reputation. It has been accused of stealing sheep, goats, cats, and poultry. Some of these accusations are not true. An eagle may carry off a lamb or a newborn goat. But an adult goat or sheep would be much too heavy even for this powerful bird. If an eagle eats one of these animals, it was probably already dead. Then the eagle would be able to divide the carcass up and carry it away in pieces.

In Austria, a country of mountains and pastures, people have made large massacres of eagles. Invariably, these massacres were followed by an increase in sickness among domestic animals and an overpopulation of snakes. As with all predators, the bird of prey mostly attacks weak or ill animals. It thereby contributes to keeping herds in good health. When it is hungry, the eagle often eats snakes, rats, and decaying animals, too.

Eagles have a very important role in the balance of nature. Their forbidding looks, crooked beaks, and steely talons have made people have misconceptions about them. With ignorance added in, these birds are among the most menaced species in the world.

A popular, but mistaken, idea about eagles.

Can you tell what a bird eats by looking at its beak?

The beak of the monk vulture.

Birds eat seeds, insects, shellfish, worms, and meat. Examining their beaks can reveal the contents of their diet.

Birds of prey, which tear up their food, have powerful, hooked beaks. If chickens are raised on meat alone, their beaks will become hooked like that of a bird of prey.

The cuckoo, which mainly eats large, hard seeds, has a beak with a wide base. The cuckoo uses the point of its beak for climbing.

Woodpeckers have long, straight beaks that are sharp at the ends. They use them for hollowing out trees in search of insects or larvae.

Herons have beaks that are useful in catching fish. The heron's beak is long and in the shape of a spear.

Birds that eat small insects have long, slender beaks that can probe and pluck the insects from cracks in trees.

Finches, sparrows, and grosbeaks have short, strong bills used for cracking hard shells of seeds.

Spoonbills and flamingoes have flat or curved beaks which make it possible for them to scrape the bottom of a swamp where they find small animals.

Darwin's finches

When Charles Darwin, the famous naturalist, discovered the animals of the Galápagos Islands in the nineteenth century, he was surprised by the variety of finches. The different varieties had very different beaks. Some were seed-eaters. Some ate insects, and some ate larvae. The diversity of beaks corresponded to the diversity of their diets. From his studies, Darwin developed his ideas known as "natural selection" or "the survival of the fittest." This is a process in nature by which the organisms best suited to their environment are the ones that will survive.

The green woodpecker and its long beak.

Notice the curved beak of the pink flamingo.

How can snakes swallow animals larger than themselves?

The giant anaconda, the largest snake of the Americas, may be more than 26 feet (8 m) long, but its neck is barely bigger than that of a man. Nevertheless, it easily eats wild pigs and alligators. The record is held by the reticulate python of the Indies, the longest snake in the world. It easily attacks and eats boars and deer.

How can the snake, with its tiny head, swallow such large beasts? Its jaw can distend in a remarkable manner. Between the upper and lower jaws of snakes, there is an elongated bone. The ligaments which connect the bones are very elastic, allowing the mouth to open in an extremely wide manner.

The snake swallows its prey whole. It has killed it beforehand by poisoning it with a bite from its venomous fangs or suffocating it in its coils. The entire victim is swallowed—hair, feathers, scales, hooves, and horns. The snake's teeth are curved inward. Once it has started to swallow, it must continue.

Once the prey has been swallowed, it travels to the stomach. Snakes have mobile sides. They can adjust themselves to make room for large prey. Snakes' stomachs possess the most powerful digestive juices that exist. This is necessary to overcome all the hard and indigestible things in a snake's diet—horns, teeth, bones, etc. Digestion is slow and laborious.

After eating, a snake may lie in the sun. The warmth speeds up the digestive process by raising the snake's body temperature.

A large prey may serve as a meal for a snake for several weeks. Large snakes, such as boas and pythons, often go without food for more than a year. Some small snakes may even go without food from six months to a year.

Snakes can survive without food for extended periods because they do not need a lot of food energy to maintain their body temperatures. Snakes may also be inactive for long periods of time and do not need a lot of food energy. They also store fat on their bodies, which they can live on during fasts.

Because snakes eat rodents, reptiles, and insects, they are useful predators.

In countries such as China and Japan, snake meat is eaten by people.

Snake venom has many uses in medicine and biological research. The medicine that is used to treat snakebite is made from blood serum of horses that have been injected with venom.

A snake digesting a large fish.

Snakes have two ways of killing. If they are poisonous snakes, they paralyze the prey with venom. If they are not poisonous snakes, they strangle the prey in their coils.

Are some insects harmful?

Only a small percentage of the eight hundred thousand species of insects are harmful. There are just a few hundred serious pests in the United States.

These insects injure or destroy almost every type of plant in existence.

Major pests in the United States include the boll weevil (which damages cotton), the Hessian fly (which attacks wheat), the corn earworm and chinch bug (which destroy corn and other crops), and the Colorado beetle (which feeds on potatoes). The processionary pine tree caterpillar is also a menace. When it enters a forest, it quickly defoliates the trees.

Many types of beetles are harmful. They graze on leaves and hollow out tunnels in wood. Their larvae are the most injurious of all. Often their larval stage is longer than their adult life. During this period, the larva sheds its skin several times, grows enormously, and accumulates reserves of food. Always hungry, the vegetarian larva causes a lot of damage.

Red ants construct anthills under the trees in the shape of enormous cones of twigs which contain several million ants. One single anthill of red ants consumes more than ten thousand beetles and caterpillars a day.

An overabundance of ants makes the soil too acid for certain plants because the ants secrete a venom which contains an acid. When the soil is too acidic, the plants that make up the undergrowth of the forests grow poorly.

Many insects are harmful indoors. Termites attack things made from wood including the structures of buildings. Clothes moths eat fabric and furs. Carpet beetles ruin carpeting and upholstery. Silverfish destroy books. Food is sometimes attacked by flies, ants, and cockroaches.

Flies, lice, and parasites harm people and animals. Certain flies and mosquitoes can spread terrible diseases.

Various methods are used to control harmful insects. Mosquito breeding grounds are drained. Government inspectors search luggage and shipments to prevent insect pests from entering the country.

Better farming techniques such as crop rotation have been implemented. Predators of the insect pests can be brought in. Often, insecticides are used.

Are insecticides dangerous only to insects?

Insecticides are poisons. Some are believed unharmful to people, domestic animals, and other vertebrates, but their accumulation may bring about disaster.

Several years ago, certain ponds were frequented by numerous aquatic birds. Wading birds, cranes, and ducks all made their nests in the reeds.

Their flight and their songs animated the ponds. But airplanes arrived and powdered the surface of the water with insecticides to kill mosquito larvae. Mosquito larvae are eaten by small crustaceans and freshwater snails which, in turn, are eaten by the birds. The poison accumulated in the birds' bodies, and they died.

As for mosquitoes, they got used to the poison. In spite of stronger and stronger doses of insecticide,

A pond is home for numerous living creatures.

A plane spreading insecticide.

they resisted. The birds continued to die and, with them, the fish, snails, crustaceans, and frogs which ate the insects and their larvae.

Insecticides generally used are non-specific. They kill all insects, the good and the bad without discrimination such as the bee (which gives us honey) and the the ladybug (which eats so many aphids).

Insecticides should be limited to desperate cases such as epidemics brought on by insects or to serious menaces of harvests which could bring famine.

Bathing buffaloes, beware!

What is a parasite?

In the nineteenth century, plant lice emanating from America endangered French wine-making. The remedy also came from America—vine plants whose sap was unpleasant to the parasite.

A parasite, whether it is animal or vegetable, lives at the expense of its living host. The big difference between predators and parasites is that predators kill their prey to eat it, while parasites have no interest in seeing their prey die. The prey's death would bring about their own.

Cercaria, which are small larvae of parasite worms, will swim toward a bathing buffalo and penetrate its body by piercing the buffalo's skin.

After a few moments, all the cercaria in the area have entered the buffalo. Until the next hatching, in about three hours, people can swim without fear. They will not risk being filled with parasites by these worms.

In the bovine (cow) family, the worm installs itself in the liver, the kidneys, and the lungs, where it eats.

A type of amoeba destroys the lining of people's intestines. This creates the disease known as amoebic dysentery. Other protozoans can cause malaria and Texas cattle fever in mammals.

Tapeworms attach themselves to the intestinal walls of a host, depriving the host of nourishment. Some ticks spread Rocky Mountain fever. Mosquitoes carry yellow fever. Lice transmit typhus. The tsetse fly carries African sleeping sickness.

Plant parasites can cause disease in people, animals, and plants. Mistletoe is only partially parasitic because it makes some of its own food. Most bacteria are parasites.

As a general rule, parasites have a preference for their host. A mammal parasite cannot develop in a bird's organism. Pork parasites cannot live in a human. When plant lice attacked vine plants in France, they were pulled up and replaced with American vines, which resist this parasite.

THE TRAVELS OF ANIMALS

A refreshing pause for migrating impalas.

An arctic tern prepares to land.

What animal is the greatest traveler in the world?

The arctic tern, a bird of the same family as seagulls, is not afraid to fly great distances.

It may lay its eggs and raise its young at the North Pole when the sun stays above the horizon all day and night. It spends winter at the South Pole, where it finds the insomniac sun once again. In this manner, it makes the most of the sun—twenty-four hours a day for eight months of the year.

This great privilege is only attained by the strength of its wings because it must make a minimum round trip of 24,800 miles (40,000 km). That is the minimum because it cannot follow an ideally straight line from one pole to the other.

Arctic terns that hatch in Labrador (Canada) fly to South Africa for the first time at age three months. They make the journey every August thereafter for the rest of their lives. The life span of the arctic tern is nearly thirty years. They fly back to Labrador every spring to breed. Although it uses to the full its gliding faculties, it must rest from time to time to eat.

Of all the terns, the arctic tern is the one that lays its eggs in the most northern areas. The young are born covered with tightly-woven down and are fed with fish and waste predigested by their parents.

How do birds find their way during migration?

When people travel, they take maps along. Sailors, who don't have marked roads or signal lights, must navigate with instruments like the sextant, the compass, and long and complicated calculations.

The small garden warblers, which migrate to South Africa in winter, find their way without a sextant, compass, map, or calculations.

A secret revealed

Evidently, warblers have a kind of sixth sense which uses the stars as points of reference to find the migratory route.

Other migrating birds may travel during the day. These birds use the sun. For them, finding their way is done with as much ease and subconsciousness as we use when sighting the top of a mountain. Their brains possess the same power as people's do—that of being able to see and understand.

Not all kinds of birds migrate, but there are certain birds in every part of the world that do.

North American birds generally use routes referred to as the *four flyways*. The *Pacific Flyway* runs along the west coast. The *Central Flyway* follows the Rockies. The *Mississippi Flyway* is located along the Mississippi River. The *Atlantic Flyway* runs along the east coast.

The government in the United States has set up waterfowl sanctuaries along these routes so that migrating birds may rest from time to time during their migration.

Birds are not the only animals that migrate. Crustaceans, locusts, butterflies, bats, and several kinds of fish achieve regular migration, often of great distances.

A garden warbler feeding her young.

Which animal makes the shortest voyages?

Tightly gripping the rock, the edge of its shell embedded in the spot it has chosen for shelter, the limpet is well known to those who frequent ocean beaches. It is found in all parts of the world. Most limpets are less than 3 inches (8 cm) long. A Mexican limpet, however, may grow to 8 inches (20 cm) long.

Limpets can be easily spotted at low tide. Their shells are attached to rocks. The shells completely cover each limpet so that they are protected from seabirds. If you try to tear this marine mollusk away from its support with your fingers, you will never succeed.

The limpet belongs to the same family as snails, slugs, and winkles. This family is famous for its slowness of movement. When it moves around, it releases the suction it is creating and slides along on its round foot like a snail. The limpet grazes on small algae which it finds near its home and, stomach full, quickly returns to shelter. Its biggest excursions take it about 4 inches (10 cm) from its usual place. It knows exactly which depression in the rock is adapted to its shell during the course of its growth. If, by mistake, it finds the wrong one and sets up home near a neighbor, the neighbor will push it gently toward its correct quarters.

It is best for the limpet to shape its point of fixation as exactly as possible. This way it can create greater pressure to hold it to its position. No matter how strong the waves are, it will remain attached to the rock and will never be swept away.

The limpet is a small sea animal with a protective shell that moves only inches from home in search of food.

ANIMALS AND THEIR YOUNG

Motherly love.

Why does a kangaroo have a pouch on its stomach?

Kangaroos are part of a very ancient group of mammals—pouch mammals or marsupials. There are over 250 kinds of marsupials. Kangaroos are the largest of the family. Some grow to be more than 7 feet (2.1 m) tall.

In earlier times, long before people were on earth, there were marsupials everywhere. Now, they are only found in Australia, Tasmania, and New Guinea and include the bandicoot, cuscus, dasyure, koala, Tasmanian devil, Tasmanian wolf, and wombat. The Virginia opossum is the only marsupial that lives in the United States.

Marsupials are being eliminated little by little by the appearance of new species of mammals that are better adapted, more evolved.

People have also brought dogs, foxes, and other animals to the regions where marsupials live. These animals prey upon the marsupial population and compete with them for food. Marsupials can also be pests to farmers, and farmers eliminate them. Hunters kill kangaroos for food and hides.

Today, the Australian government is trying to protect the kangaroo.

The opossum in the United States is not in danger because opossums will eat almost any type of food. They also have a high rate of reproduction.

The pouch which characterizes a marsupial is a fold in the skin on its stomach. It can open in the front or in the back. Hidden by this fold of skin are the mammaries.

A newborn "larva"

The offspring of marsupials are very different from their parents when they are just born. For example, the adult red kangaroo has a very powerful tail and hind legs for jumping, very short forepaws, and a head that slightly resembles a rabbit's. But its young has rear paws that are barely formed and robust forepaws armed with claws. In fact, newborn marsupials are still embryos. Nevertheless, these embryos have nervous systems developed enough for them to bring about the projection necessary to leave the mother's womb and enter the marsupial pouch.

The female kangaroo carries her young five to six weeks. At its birth, the baby measures 2-3 inches (6-7 cm). Babies drink the milk from the bodies of their mothers. At the age of six months, a baby looks like a miniature kangaroo and begins to make some small excursions outside the pouch. But it does not leave this shelter altogether until it is a year old.

The kangaroo's pouch is both a sort of nest in which the embryo finishes developing and a shelter for the baby. When there is danger, the young kangaroo jumps into the mother's pouch.

A baby wallaby in its mother's marsupial pouch.

A very busy opossum.

How do birds learn to build their nests?

Most birds build nests to hold their eggs and their young.

Birds don't *learn* how to build their nests. They know how instinctively. Instinct is a behavior that is inherited rather than learned.

Young birds automatically know how to build nests that conform to the model built by their species. The art of constructing the cradle for their young is not a learned technique but a technique already written into their hereditary program.

There are many different varieties of nests. The simplest may be a pile of sticks and other items on the ground. Water birds often use pebbles and grass to make a nest. Tree nests have to be very strong to resist bad weather. Some birds weave nests out of grass and palm leaves.

Woodpeckers dig holes in the trunks of dead trees and make their nests inside. Some birds build nests in chimneys. The nests are made of twigs and the birds' saliva. Mound birds make nests by piling soil and dead plants.

Birds' innate memories

It is people who must *learn* almost everything necessary in order to live. The innate memories of birds are both marvelous and mysterious. Imagine how life would be simplified if people could inherit from their parents the ability to speak several languages.

Instinct varies

Animals that do not have a high capacity for learning (such as insects, spiders, and crustaceans) rely almost completely on instinct.

A water bird building its nest.

A weaver weaving the cradle for its future offspring.

The rudimentary nest of a seagull.

Higher animals (fish, birds, and mammals) have the capacity to learn more. Instinctive behaviors can also be changed through learning. These animals can depend less on instinct.

Fish rely more on instinct than birds. Birds use more instinct than mammals.

Humans, as infants, behave instinctively. But as adults, most behavior is learned.

A robin exhausts herself feeding an enormous baby cuckoo.

How does the cuckoo get other birds to raise its young?

The gray cuckoo (about 14 inches or 35 cm long) lives throughout Europe and in the temperate and subtropical zones of Africa and Asia. Cuckoos of the northern regions spend winters in Africa. They mostly feed on caterpillars and insects.

Nests are really only cradles to birds. There the eggs are laid and hatched. A nest is never used as shelter or a resting place for an adult bird.

Some species of cuckoos build nests for themselves. Other cuckoos, however, behave in a way that destroys other birds. When certain cuckoo mothers feel that the moment of laying is near, they look for a pleasant nest for the offspring.

Many species of cuckoos are parasitic. They lay each of their eggs in nests belonging to other birds.

When a cuckoo is ready to lay, she finds an appropriate nest (usually a songbird's). She picks up one of the songbird's eggs with her bill and then lays one of her own eggs in its place. She either swallows the egg she picked up or drops and breaks it. Then the mother cuckoo leaves.

In some curious way, hormones and a hereditary characteristic make the cuckoo's eggs look quite similar to those of the builders of the nest. If a cuckoo chooses to continuously invade a nest of warblers, her eggs will come to resemble more and more the eggs of the warbler. At hatching time, the baby cuckoo gets rid of other eggs in the nest or its nestmates (if there are any) and is fed by its adoptive parents.

ANIMALS AND PEOPLE

A child with a monkey.

Buffalo Bill after the hunt.

Have people brought about the disappearance of animal species?

Yes. Since people have been on earth, living species have disappeared—birds, mammals, insects, and plants.

There have been massacres of animals during the course of abusive hunts of the kind that Buffalo Bill undertook. He and his accomplices prided themselves on having slaughtered more than twenty thousand bison.

Ignorance has brought on the demise of animals that were misinterpreted as being harmful. Monetary gain has brought about a dangerous shortage of many types of fur-coated animals. And then there is human civilization itself which has changed the surroundings and the natural habitat, eliminating certain species. Sometimes their food is poisoned by pesticides, and the animals die or become infertile.

Today, conservationists carefully take a census of endangered animals. These animals are protected, but sometimes it is already too late. More than thirty species of nocturnal and diurnal birds of prey are nearly extinct. For them, the laws of protection have come too late. Only zoos preserve some very rare animals and often only for a little while because they don't reproduce well in captivity.

Can an extinct species be brought back?

Most books about paleontology, the study of fossils, show splendid and terrifying drawings of extraordinary reptiles which lived on the earth hundreds of millions of years ago. These reptiles were the *diplodocus, tyrannosaurus,* and *stegosaurus.* By using skeletons, footprints, eggs, and other things preserved in the earth, specialists have been able to reconstruct the general appearance of these animals, their habits, and their food. Baron Georges Cuvier was the first, at the beginning of the nineteenth century, to reconstruct these extinct species.

Throughout time, people have contributed to the disappearance of a great many animal species by hunting and by destroying their source of food and their natural habitat. Now there are laws to protect a species that is in danger of extinction. It is improbable that one day an extinct species will thrive again.

Nevertheless, in one case in particular, a team of zoologists obtained some remarkable results.

The aurochs is a bovine species that is extinct today. Yet, some privileged zoos boast of possessing some aurochs couples. Where have they come from? Aurochs, which used to be very widespread in Europe, Asia, and North Africa, gave birth to diverse races of domestic cattle. Because the last one died in Poland in 1627, there are still many drawings, descriptions, and several relatively well-preserved skeletons which give an idea of their appearance. Armed with these documents, zoologists have reconstructed the aurochs through its different descendants. It had large horns, curved forward, with black points. These horns reappeared in a race of Hungarian cattle. The Asian zebu has one or two aurochs characteristics. From there, different bovine races were selected and crossbred. Researchers studying these animals eventually found themselves in the possession of a couple of young aurochs-appearing animals. These animals, in turn, gave birth to real aurochs.

This discovery created controversy. The animals born resemble the drawings of aurochs, but are they really aurochs? Do they have the entire hereditary program of these disappeared bovines?

Top: A diplodocus. *Below:* A stegosaurus.

Below: Hunting aurochs.

How are animals in nature studied?

For a long time, naturalists have gathered plants, animals, and minerals and studied them carefully in their laboratories.

Anthills have been transported from their natural sites to plaster or glass habitations where they can be easily studied. Butterfly chrysalises are carefully "hatched" in order to observe the emergence of the adult insect. Generations of flies are raised in bottles where they are studied. Important information about these animals can be obtained in this way.

Scientists also have the immense task of studying animals in their natural habitat. These scientists are called ecologists. *Ecology* means the science of the habitat. It is since 1930 that ecology has fully developed. An ecologist is a combination of a naturalist, a biologist, a chemist, a physician, and more. The study of ecology brings about understanding of the world and all that it possesses. This knowledge is essential to the well-being of all living things on earth.

Some ecologists study air and water pollution and how it affects people, animals, and vegetation. They try to foresee problems and offer solutions.

Ecologists also are working on the problem of the earth's dwindling natural resources such as coal, gas, and oil. They are studying the uses of solar energy.

The world's increasing population and decreasing food supply is another concern of ecologists.

Young people who are interested in observing nature, who are astonished by the colors of flowers and butterflies that hover around them, who have respect for the tranquility of animals, who love nature and want to learn to understand and preserve it, and who are attentive and have an eye for detail will make good ecologists.

Zoos and aquariums

Zoos and aquariums are places where wildlife can be observed by the public.

Scientists and ecologists can also study the animals there in a controlled environment. It is also an important place for endangered wildlife to breed.

It isn't known when the first zoos and aquariums came into existence. Pigeons were kept in captivity as early as 4500 B.C. in Iraq.

Ecologists at work in a forest.

A puffin reserve on the Atlantic coast.

What is a reserve?

A penguin reserve.

A penguin reserve.

Reserves or refuges are vast expanses of land set aside or "reserved" for animals and plants. All plants and animals are protected there, and contact with humans is reduced to discreet observation.

Some reserves are part of national parks. There are also specialized reserves which protect endangered species. Certain birds have preferred nesting areas, and it is necessary to stop people's instrusion in these areas.

California established the first bird sanctuary in the United States, Lake Merritt in Oakland, in 1870.

National wildlife refuges in the United States are open to the public, but visitors must respect the rules that protect the wildlife.

An African elephant is seen destroying the vegetation of its habitat.

What happens when animals become too numerous or dangerous in a reserve?

When animals are taken from the wild and placed in a controlled environment, problems of a different type can occur. Their natural predators are not around. Therefore, there is nothing to restrict the increase in population. They become more and more numerous over time.

Certain animals may become harmful to those around them in a reserve if they are too numerous. The ease with which they receive a constant supply of food may incite them to waste.

In certain African reserves, elephants have become too numerous.

They disobey the laws of the herd, uproot trees, and tear up bushes. If they were allowed to continue, they would end up turning the vast spaces they inhabit into deserts.

In nature, everything is a question of balance. If balance is destroyed, catastrophes will happen. Specialists are the only ones who can judge the gravity of each particular situation and determine what measures to take. Often, they capture excess animals and send them elsewhere. In this way, a balance is achieved in the controlled environment of the reserve.

How do the animals themselves control their population?

Small round worms attack cereals like wheat. The female pricks the flower and lays her eggs in it. Then a black swelling develops, overflowing with parasites instead of golden wheat. But a mushroom which branches out under the soil by forming knots is a big enemy of these worms. As soon as one of them bites a knot, it swells up and the worm is immobilized, killed, and slowly digested.

In the world, the animals themselves govern their population. Three major factors can influence the size of the population.

First, territoriality occurs among animals that require a certain minimum amount of space. Among these species, one group establishes a territory. This guarantees that the strongest members of the population will find food and have offspring.

Secondly, dominance hierarchies or pecking orders occur among social animals. The stronger animals dominate the weaker ones in the search for food, shelter, and breeding places.

Stress occurs when animals are crowded. They become irritable and aggressive, and they fight each other. In this type of situation, some individuals do not breed at all or produce smaller than average litters. Many mothers do not take care of their young, and some even eat their young. Diseases and parasites spread rapidly in a crowded situation.

Have modern times benefited from the study of animals?

Inventions are numerous in the high-tech world of today. There are many things in nature that resemble modern invention.

Animals and sonar

For a long time, naturalists have been intrigued by the way bats avoid obstacles in the dark. Sonar works on the same principles allowing humans to maneuver without visibility. A sonar device sends out a signal that is inaudible to the human ear. The time the sound takes to go and come back makes it possible to calculate the distance of the obstacle. Bats' moving and uttering cries that are inaudible to human ears allow them to locate obstacles in their paths. Whales and dolphins also use sonar. Researchers are currently studying the possibility of making a sonar device to guide the blind.

Animals and airplanes

Since the beginning of time, people have envied birds their ability to fly. For centuries, people tried to copy these fliers until they eventually succeeded. A bird and an airplane can fly for the same reasons. A bird is able to fly mainly because the pressure of the air on top of its wings is less than the pressure beneath its wings.

When a birds' wings move forward in flight, the air must travel farther and faster over the curved top surface of the wings than it does over the bottom surface. Therefore, the pressure on top of the wing is less than below.

Scientists have learned a great deal from birds. Aerodynamics (the motion of air and other forces acting on objects in motion) is a field that has developed due to the study of birds in flight.

A dolphin leaping in the open sea.

Scientists in need of solutions to problems look to see how the animals and plants have resolved the same problems.

Animals and submarines
The engineers who built submarines wanted to make them more resistant and faster. So they undertook a study of porpoises.

Porpoises can dive to vast depths and move at about 22 miles (35 km) per hour. How can they travel so quickly? Biologists and physicians teamed up to study the amazing porpoises.

The submarines of the future may be enveloped in a supple outer layer and have an elastic tail to gain the advantages that the porpoise has.

A skin diver studies the way dolphins swim.

The marvelous eye of a toad.

What is the best way to live in harmony with animals?

To love an animal is to understand it. The youngest and most inexperienced of mothers understands quickly what her baby needs. In order to understand animals, just observe and appreciate them.

Some animals, at first sight, have an odd appearance. The toad does not seem like a great beauty. But take the time to see that the toad's eyes are magnificent. The toad's iris is brilliantly colored and so deep that the poets of ancient times imagined them to be precious stones.

A toad is timid, never menacing. Its skin secretes a poison, but that is its only protection. People of bygone days often used the venom of a toad in medicinal remedies.

Toads do people a service by eating insects and slugs.

Sloths are mammals that inhabit the tropical forests of South and Central America. They hang downward from branches. Sloths have a very odd appearance. They have almost no tails or ears, and their noses are blunt. Their hair is long and coarse.

Some people think the sloth is lazy because it moves so slowly— 1/3 mile (.5 km) per hour when it moves at all. But there is a good explanation for this. The sluggishness is due, in part, to an extremely low body temperature.

To live in harmony with animals, get to know more about them and the many qualities they possess. By observing animals, you will discover their beauty, visible or hidden. They will always teach you something new.

Glossary

adaptation   modification of an organism to make it more suitable to its environment.

aerodynamics   the motion of air and other forces acting on objects in motion.

ancestor   a person from whom another person is descended.

batrachians   a vertebrate amphibian such as a frog or toad.

botanist   a scientist who studies plant life.

carnivorous   feeding and subsisting on animal tissues.

carrion   dead and rotting flesh upon which certain animals feed.

cavernal   existing in a cave or hollow away from the sunlight.

cold-blooded   having a body temperature that varies according to the temperature of the surroundings. Reptiles are cold-blooded animals.

descendants   proceeding from an ancestor or source.

diurnal   relating to or occurring in the daytime.

dromedary   a one-humped camel known for its unusual speed. Dromedaries are often bred and trained for riding.

drought   a prolonged period of time without rain that causes extensive damage to crops.

ecologist   a person who studies the interrelationships of organisms with their environments.

edentate   mammals that have few or no teeth. Edentates include the sloth, armadillo, and anteater.

endangered   threatened with extinction.

environment   the surroundings or external physical conditions affecting the growth and development of organisms.

ganglion   a cluster of nerve cells that form a nerve center.

genus   a group of animals that have common characteristics.

girth   a measurement around the body of a human or animal.

herbivorous   feeding and subsisting on plants.

hereditary   genetically transmitted from parent to offspring.

hibernation   passing the winter in an inactive or dormant state.

larva   the immature form that hatches from the egg of many insects that eventually transforms into a pupa from which the adult emerges.

lethargic   the state of being sluggish.

lineage   individuals tracing descent from a common ancestor.

mammal   any of a class of higher vertebrates comprising humans and all other animals that nourish their young with milk from the mother's mammary glands.

marine   relating to the sea.

marsupial   mammals such as kangaroos, wombats, bandicoots, and opossums that have a pouch on the abdomen of the female to carry the young.

natural selection   a theory developed by Charles Darwin defining a process in nature by which the organisms best suited to their environment are the ones that will survive.

nocturnal   relating to or occurring in the night.

paleontology   the study of fossils.

phosphorescent   exhibiting a luminescence that is caused by absorption of radiation that continues for a time after the radiation has ended.

phyla   primary divisions of the animal kingdom.

predator   an animal that hunts and kills other animals for food.

pupa   a cocoon; an intermediate stage in the transformation of a larva into an adult.

reserve   a vast expanse of land set aside for animals and plants.

scavenger   an organism that feeds on garbage or carrion.

sonar   a means to detect the presence and location of objects by the reflection of sonic and supersonic waves.

species   a basic unit of scientific classification that groups together individuals having common attributes and designated by a common name.

unicellular   having or consisting of a single cell.

warm-blooded   having a high and constant body temperature regardless of the surroundings.

wingspan   the distance from the tip of one wing to the tip of the other.

zoologist   a scientist who studies the animal kingdom.

INDEX